Show Me Millions!

The story of Floyd Mayweather Jr.

Tom Cruise's 1996 film Jerry Maguire where he played a sports agent was like opening a door and seeing piles of gold inside. Film makers may not have known it but they were helping to usher in a world going one way. Up, then UP some more.

The familiar world of everyday sport and sports fans was transforming into a trillion dollar business.

Sport became the sport business, sportsmen became global figures then multi millionaires. While at that moment - Floyd Mayweather Jr was just starting out on his boxing career.

In the film, agent Jerry Maguire struggled with his ideals and his sports business was losing out. But the jubilant style of last remaining client Rod Tidwell, played by Cuba Gooding Jr, changed Jerry's luck.

Chanting his mantra *"Show me the money – show me the money"* Rod Tidwell forced Maguire to join in the chant and after he did, told him

"Congratulations – you're still my agent".

In real life Floyd Mayweather was listening, taking it all in. Nobody knows what happens in this story. He is already the richest athlete in the world and there is still untapped wealth in sponsorships waiting for Floyd outside the ring. He is a phenomenon, a money machine like no other. Is that enough for him? His whole life and family are steeped in boxing culture. In his post fight interviews with commentator Larry Merchant he shows his irritation when he is accused of being boring and not giving the fans the value their money deserves.

So no, it's not enough. He wants to be remembered as the greatest boxer of all time. Although he will also say, 'I'm not into legends, I'm in the cheque cashing business.'

But he is the game changer who has to operate by himself. Boxing pulls in the biggest crowds, creates the biggest heroes when there are feuds as well as fights. Mohammad Ali and Joe Frazier for example, Sugar Ray Leonard against Tommy Hearns, Sugar Ray Robinson and Jake Lamotta.

So far the Money Man has a big feud – but no fight – and that's not enough. So will Mayweather – Pacquiao ever happen?

One day. Maybe.

"Some pay to see me win, some pay to see me lose, but they all pay"

Floyd Mayweather Jr.

Floyd's first ever professional fight in 1996 was a hurdle he jumped over with some ease. His opponent, Roberto Apodaca, was the traditional journeyman fighter and he went down in 37 seconds of the second round to a body shot. Floyd looked a bit wild, we didn't see fast hands but we did see real power. At featherweight he was a big puncher and the left hook that dropped Apodaca was a finisher. Just in case it was needed, Floyd's right was on it's way.

Pretty Boy Floyd looked pretty but most of all he did look young. With Uncle Roger in attendance he was quiet, respectful. Eager to please his after fight interviewer. Jumping forward to his fifth fight against 33 year old Kino Rodriguez, there was a showboating difference. Attitude was the word commentators picked up on and he made his opponent, a man with nine wins on his record, look bad. Gone was the respect and in one minute 44 seconds - gone was Rodriguez. As he moved his hands up to protect his head against the combinations pouring in, Pretty Boy hit him with a left hook to the ribs that sent him on his way for a TKO.

Afterwards boxing insiders made the point that young fighters often don't appreciate the value of body shots. But then not many have the fighting background of Floyd Jr. His father Floyd Sr. was a welterweight contender, his uncle Jeff a former IBO super featherweight champion, and Uncle Roger is a former WBC super-lightweight champion. Floyd Jr inherited the genes together with a whole ring full of trouble. Floyd Sr had a violent temper and wandering ways. He was shot in the leg by the brother of a girlfriend – while he was holding young Floyd in his arms. Later he served time for dealing in cocaine. Floyd Jr has also served time for assaulting his wife. But troubled personal lives run as a continuing thread through boxing history.

One theory is that the Alpha male personality, plus the boxer's need to dominate, does as much harm to personal relationships - as it helps them in the ring. Floyd's problems have led to a constant theme in boxing forums, love the boxer, hate the man. But not all the boxing community condemned him for his troubles. There were jokes too as in this supposed conversation between the judge and Mayweather.

Judge, 'Tell me Mr Mayweather, why do you keep beating your wife'?

Mayweather, 'I think it's my superior footwork sir'.

Floyd's overpowering personality inside and outside the ring was building steadily right through his early fights. Fast hands, dancing feet and physical power carried him along. Constant training and gym work shaped his body and his fighter's heart. This was a young man who had been in the gym since he was around six, whose grandmother first spotted his potential. There was no Ricky Hatton style deviation from training between fights, Floyd was always in the gym, ready to go.

After 10 fights, 10 wins and 9 KO's, he climbed into the ring with Felipe Garcia a tough Mexican with 10 wins but plenty of defeats. He had been around a long time and was one of those fighters who usually went the distance. Garcia could make an opponent look bad with his hard to hit, swaying, bouncing moves. Could he do the same to Floyd?

Not a chance. Floyd caught him in the sixth with a left hook to the chin followed by three straight rights. He was stretched out and as the commentator said, 'He's going to have trouble getting up'. That's what the referee thought too and he stopped the fight.

After this eleventh fight the Mayweather reputation was building inside and outside the ring. Boxing thrives on characters, the ones with spice in their personality. We're not talking banking here – this is boxing . Alongside the boxing talent a big money making champion needs the ability to communicate. He has to build the fan base himself through the force of his personality. If they can't be fans, well haters are useful too!

The great Sugar Ray Leonard has pointed up one of the attractions of the Mayweather circus saying Floyd brings people who aren't interested in the sport - into boxing. He talks street rap, never lost for a word. What Sugar Ray didn't say of course was that maybe half of the Mayweather followers could be haters.

For them Floyd can do no right, they tune in to see him get beaten. Boxing is a sport like no other in the way it divides opinion. Hard core fans worship a perfectionist like Mayweather. The haters are just as strong in their feeling. They crowd onto boxing forums and comment on YouTube videos, pouring out fire.

"I Think What Floyd Mayweather Jr Is Doing Is Awesome"

Sugar Ray Leonard speaking after Mayweather stopped Ricky Hatton

Maybe it is because boxing is one of the most primitive of sports that fighters attract such widely varying opinions. Lovers and haters are equally extreme. But as a spectator sport boxing is also a release. In the wider society physical aggression isn't going away, now or in the future. Boxing puts the aggression into an arena where it can be safely enjoyed. Professionals work out the fantasies of the spectators, taking the pain, doing the fighting.

Roman emperors knew the value of gladiatorial contests where the events were a diversion for the crowds, a spectacle and a reward for citizens who went about their daily lives in peace. In a twisted way the contests were more honest than some Vegas bouts. No worries about referees or fixed fights. Brutality ruled and that mob, ancestors of The Mob, usually went home happy.

Bread and circuses were seen as the foundations of a calm society. The idea doesn't work today but boxing has definitely earned a place in society. There isn't the high profile enjoyed in the golden days of Muhammad Ali or the young Mike Tyson but the gold is still there as Money Mayweather never stops reminding one and all.

Floyd Jr would see himself as both Emperor on the podium – and gladiator in the ring. That is the status he believes he should have and in many ways he's achieved it. He selects his opponents and grants them some time in the ring. They leave battered, bruised, defeated – but a lot richer. No one rules the sport like Mayweather. He knows it and makes sure everyone else does too.

There is of course one boxer who doesn't fit into the pattern as Floyd sees it, Manny Pacquiao. He is the mystery ingredient in the Mayweather story and for the moment, it's an unsolved mystery.

At the beginning of his career, Mayweather Jr had a raft of journeymen fighters to work through. These are the fighters who started out with high hopes but as time and defeats pile up, they become journeymen. A skilled tradesman with no prospects who is paid to fatten a genuine contender's record.

No fighter starts out wanting to be a journeyman. He begins with hopes of a crack at a title but through lack of talent – or support from promoters – he falls down the ratings. Or he is cheated out of success. Hollywood has given us plenty of examples. 'I could have been a contender' says Marlon Brando as Terry Malloy in that iconic scene from *On The Waterfront* as he chats to his brother in the back of a taxi. His brother managed his career but sold him short and persuaded him to throw a fight he could have won. A boxer like Terry Malloy would finish as a journeyman, fighting for thin rewards.

That was never going to happen to a stand out talent and fierce competitor like young Floyd. His father's career faltered but that just made Floyd more determined.

Back in 1998 Mayweather was learning his ringcraft and growing his reputation. He was fighting boxers like Sam Girard who may have been in a division above Floyd but was not really in his league. Girard's career record was won 17, lost 7, respectable enough but he got out of the ring at just 26. His two rounds with Floyd may well have contributed to that decision. Down in the first round, he was on the floor – and smiling – in the second. He got up but after another onslaught went down head first and the referee stopped it.

Two Boxers Shot – One Was A Mayweather

Grand Rapids Michigan has a pedigree in boxing. The Mayweather clan including young Floyd grew up there but before them there was another world champion. He started young like Floyd and at the beginning of the last century he was a world champion at just 20. This was Stanley Ketchell, World Middleweight Champion and known as the Missouri Assassin. Many judged him to be one of the hardest punchers the world has seen.

Ketchell was fighting all comers in boxing booths at 16 and working as a bouncer in between fights. As he said at the time, he didn't get into boxing just because he liked the money. Stanley enjoyed the fighting too.

So much so that he would take on men from the heavier divisions, sometimes without thinking to think about it.

His opponents included World Heavyweight Champion Jack Johnson who he fought – and knocked down. That wasn't supposed to happen. The two men had agreed to make the fight last at least 20 rounds to maximise their money from filming. But Ketchell, who had taken real punishment in the fight, wanted to finish it. He did, but not in the way he hoped. Johnson was so enraged he got up from the canvas and knocked Ketchell out with a single punch, leaving several of his teeth embedded in his glove.

The next 12 months were devastating for Ketchell and at the end of them he was dead. The Mayweather family has seen some turbulent times but not as bad as this. Ketchell made $100,000 fighting, at least $2.4 million by today's standards but he spent money even faster than Floyd.

The hard times began when he lost a guiding influence, his manager died unexpectedly after the Johnson fight. The champion started drinking heavily and lost his championship belt – not in the ring but in a hotel room in Chicago. Studded with diamonds and valued at $29,000 today, Ketchell never got it back.

Later he dreamed up a scheme to prevent white hope Jim Jeffries being humiliated against Jack Johnson. He decided that when he was introduced inn the ring before the fight, instead of shaking hands with Jeffries he would knock him out. Promoter Tex Rickard heard about the plan and made sure it never happened.

Tragedy struck when Ketchell was trying to regain his health and some peace at the ranch of a family friend in Missouri. Helping out at the ranch were a couple named Walter Hurtz and Goldie Smith. Ketchell was eating a breakfast made by Smith when Hurtz came in and shot him in the back. It was never established whether it was a botched robbery attempt or revenge by Hurtz because Ketchell had an affair with Smith.

The famous journalist John Lardner summed up the situation like this, "Stanley Ketchel was 24 years old when he was fatally shot in the back by the common-law husband of the lady who was cooking his breakfast."

Floyd Jr was just two years old when he encountered serious violence. His father, and the brother of Floyd's mother, had a business dispute that soon escalated after Floyd Sr grabbed him by the throat and sent him on his way. But the man arrived at home where Floyd was with his father and mother – waving a shotgun. Floyd Sr grabbed his son and held him in front of him to act as a shield. The way he described it later to the LA Times, "It wasn't about putting my son in the line of fire. I knew he wouldn't kill the baby. He lowered the gun from my face and bam, he shot me in the leg."

Floyd Sr was wounded in the thigh and the injury badly affected his boxing career. He went from being a contender who took Sugar Ray Leonard to a decision, to journeyman. His life became a scramble for money.

Floyd Jr was too young to understand what was happening but he has memories of a childhood that could have destroyed him. Instead it hardened him. He was a Mayweather and he took to the gym life.

At 10 Floyd was standing on a box hitting the speed bag. In interviews he described living in desperately poor conditions in New Jersey but he was always able to escape to another home - the gym. In that punishing arena Floyd Jr learned about his future life. Family problems and tragedies never crushed his spirit. As he grew he acquired rigid discipline in training plus the vital ingredient a champion needs – self belief.

World Champion After Just Eighteen Fights And Fourteen KO's

Maybe Team Mayweather spotted something the others overlooked. After a long career WBC super featherweight champion Genaro Hernandez was there for the taking

Some thought Mayweather had come to a world title fight early. He was only 21 and although his talents and ring skills had impressed boxing's insiders – they also knew he hadn't been really tested. Hernandez was still a strong, cagey fighter. But negative thinking never fitted into the Mayweather mindset, both Floyd Jr and his manager father knew this timing was right.

Besides, Floyd Sr was back after serving five years in prison for drug offences and he was eager to take his son to a world title. He always claimed to be the one who set young Floyd off on his career, laid the foundation for everything that was to follow. In true Mayweather family style that view was hotly disputed by Floyd's uncle Roger, also a world champion who later took over from Floyd Sr after father and son fell out.

So Floyd was up for the 130lb, WBC super featherweight title. Even though the holder, Mexican American fighter Genaro Hernandez, had only been beaten once in a 14 year career. That was when he lost to the hugely talented, younger and heavier Oscar De La Hoya.

The contest pitched a 40 fight near veteran - against the latest sensation. The betting said this would be close. As Damon Runyon put it years earlier, *'The race is not always to the swift nor the battle to the strong, but that's the way to bet.'* Floyd was swift and he was strong but on the other hand, Hernandez had 38 wins with 17 KOs. He was a formidable fighter with more experience than Floyd could even think about.

Coming into the fight Floyd said at some point Hernandez would have to widen the hands he usually held up in defence – and he would punch straight through the gap. That's exactly what happened – but earlier than anyone expected.

Right from the first bell Mayweather was finding Hernandez with combinations, mixing them up, impressing George Foreman who was on commentary. The ex-champion is a shrewd observer of the fight game and he said Floyd was a natural. "It usually takes years of training before fighters can box like this", he said. Perhaps big George forgot that Floyd had been training for years, from childhood.

The fight was never as close as predicted. Hernandez could not find a way to hurt Mayweather and every time he tried young Floyd came back at him, sometimes with six punch combinations.

Going into the 8th Hernandez's brother told him in the corner, "Last round, last round." He didn't like the punishment the champion was taking and Floyd was nearly out of sight on points. George Foreman put it this way, "Hernandez got old during the fight."

The youth, strength and boxing skills of Mayweather gave the veteran nowhere to go. Time after time he tried backing onto the ropes, hoping to catch Floyd with a counter but it didn't happen. At the end of the round his corner retired him and it was the end of his career.

There is a tragic footnote to this fight. Only a few years later Hernandez was diagnosed as having a rare and fatal cancer. His treatment was not covered by insurance. Promoter Bob Arum helped with the fees but by the time the ex-champion died most of his savings were gone. Floyd Mayweather stepped in and without any publicity, paid for the funeral. He simply said, "I was just grateful he gave me the chance and it all started there. I was happy to help." A very different view of the Money Mayweather legend.

Champion Who Lost His Belt In A Pawn Shop

All too often it's a thin line between success in boxing and a career out of control, racing downhill. When Floyd Mayweather stepped into the ring for his sixth defence of the Super Featherweight title against Diego Corrales, there was a fighter on either side of that line.

Floyd was an established champion with a career founded on hard work and solid training. Focused and determined to be the best around. A natural talent but Mayweather backed it up with gym time.

Diego Corrales had enjoyed success too. At various periods he was the WBC, WBO and *The Ring* lightweight champion, the WBO and IBF super featherweight champion. Later he was given *The Ring* & Boxing Writers Association of America awards for his sensational lightweight fight against Jose Luis Castillo.

Before the Mayweather contest, Diego was undefeated over 33 fights with 27 stoppages. At his best he was a world class fighter but right now he was unprepared and despairing, facing a prison term for domestic abuse of his wife and short of money. This was a running problem for him, he could be wild outside the ring as well as inside. One of his championship belts spent time in the pawn shop before being sold at a big profit – to the pawnbroker.

Corrales only took the fight because he was desperately short of money. Mentally he wasn't ready and he was weak from making the weight. Even on the day of the fight he still had to lose a couple of lbs.

This was no time to be fighting a champion like Mayweather. Diego didn't throw enough punches, only 60 that connected throughout the fight, but his great heart kept him coming forward.

Although Floyd was estranged from his father he rang him for advice before the fight. He was told to stick and move and go for the body. Floyd followed the plan and Corrales could not catch him. Again and again Mayweather made him miss then shook him up with jabs and hooks.

By the seventh round Corrales was hopelessly behind on points and running out of gas. Mayweather put him down three times in the round but his fighter's instinct made him carry on. He was down twice in the tenth before his stepfather threw in the towel – and still Corrales protested.

Before the fight the ruthless side of Team Mayweather had come through. Floyd trash talked Diego, taunting him about his upcoming trial for abuse of his wife. Later on this would return to haunt him as he faced the identical problem. But for the moment the tactic worked, controversy raised the profile and boosted the gate.

Significantly Mayweather was rewarded with a six fight deal with HBO that would bring in $15 million. Floyd had turned down an earlier HBO offer for $12.5 for six fights, calling that a 'slave contract'. His father thought Floyd was 'nuts' to turn it down and told him so.

Mistake. By now it was Money who did the talking, his father the walking. They split up and Floyd took him off the Team Mayweather payroll. Uncle Roger took over and Floyd was proved right– a better deal came rushing down the road.

In one of those terrible twists there was tragedy waiting for Corrales. His last victory, after a monumental fight, was the sensational knock out of Jose Luis Castillo. In 2007 Diego was killed in a motor cycle accident. Once again a talented champion and great fighter met an early death.

Mayweather v Judah And The Sparring Session That Lit A Fuse

There was a time when Floyd Mayweather and Zab Judah would go clubbing together and enjoy the night. But sharing a gym and then sparring with each other was a big mistake. According to insiders at the gym the trouble started when Judah went in too heavily against a fighter Mayweather had an interest in. It led to a bad atmosphere that got rapidly worse when they started sparring. According to the Mayweather camp, Floyd punished Zab before the sparring session was stopped by their trainers, Roger Mayweather and Judah's father, Yoel.

If the sparring went badly, it was nothing compared to what happened in the ring. In the opening two rounds Zab was landing some good shots, one that knocked Floyd off his feet although the referee did not count it a knockdown. But gradually Floyd took over, his body shots were followed up by double right hands and Zab was looking more and more reluctant to launch a fightback.

The inter round instructions said it all. Roger Mayweather told Floyd to keep throwing body shots, he knew Judah was hurting and losing his way. Zab's father Yoel was slapping his son's face, saying "Listen to me man, you got to let your hands go." He knew Zab was well behind on points but as the inter round commentators said, that's easy for the trainer to say, he wasn't taking the punishment that came back every time Zab hit out.

Then in the 10th round everything went wild. Judah hit Mayweather with a low punch then followed up with one to the back of the head. It looked like frustration from Judah because he couldn't get past Mayweather's defence. Floyd was in agony as the referee stepped in. More sensationally, so did Roger Mayweather. He jumped into the ring and squared up to Zab Judah.

Not far behind, Yoel Judah climbed in to threaten Roger. Instantly it seemed like everyone from both camps was in the ring attacking each other. Police and security piled in to sort the situation out but it took a while and the ring was packed full with very angry people.

When the fight was resumed Floyd simply had to box the last two round to win but the Nevada State commissioners withheld the purses of both boxers until they had watched the video. When their verdicts were announced they came down heavily on Roger Mayweather and the Judah camp.

Zab was fined $250,000 and his licence was revoked for a year, Yoel Judah was fined $100,000 and his licence was also revoked for a year. Roger Mayweather was fined his entire paycheck for the fight, $200,000 and he lost his licence for a year. Leonard Ellerbe a prominent member of Team Mayweather and cornerman in the fight, was fined $50,000. It was a lot of money, a load of hassle – for one low blow.

Floyd kept his title and his purse. That's how it was always going to be. Zab Judah said the foul punch was an accident. Who knows? In boxing almost anything is possible.

From Cinderella Man To Golden Boy

Jim Braddock, the man who beat Max Baer to take the heavyweight crown in 1935, was the first boxer to be labelled the Cinderella Man. It was because of his rags to riches background. In the depression years he was fighting to put food on the family table and only got the chance to go in with Baer because the champion's manager thought it would be an easy payday.

Carlos Baldomir was the Cinderella Man of his times because he also struggled to make his way – until he beat Zab Judah to take his WBC welterweight title. Judah underestimated him and Baldomir fought an inspired journeyman's fight. He rattled the champion badly in the seventh to win a unanimous decision.

When Braddock defended his title against Joe Louis he was hit so hard he said afterwards it felt like a "Flashbulb going off in my face, I could have stayed down for a week."

When Baldomir took his title into the ring against Mayweather that wasn't going to happen to him. He was a tough fighter with a great chin. But he was also slow and although Floyd found it embarrassingly easy to hit him, he wasn't going to knock Baldomir out.

One reason was that his right hand was hurting badly and for the last few rounds he hardly threw it. What he did do was put on a master class of defensive boxing – while at the same time piling up the points. The Mayweather haters didn't like it but he was injured and winning easily. In despair the Baldomir corner was telling him he had to get closer, put his left foot between Floyd's and land rights.

They might as well have instructed their man to take off and fly round the ring. That was the only way Baldomir was going to catch Floyd and afterwards he admitted it, "I never fought my fight, he's too fast, I couldn't catch him." He wasn't the first and wouldn't be the last to say that.

After the Louis fight original Cinderella Man, Jim Braddock, became quite rich. That was because to get the fight for the championship the Louis camp signed an agreement to give him 10% of future earnings. An arrangement that lasted quite some time.

What are the chances of the Money Man signing a deal like that? A big fat zero - although his opponents might consider it. Because Floyd always makes money for the other guy too.

Not that his next opponent, Oscar De La Hoya, was short of money. Golden Boy may have been coming to the end of a glittering and financially rewarding career in the ring but he was replacing it with a promoter's role for some of the most lucrative fights ever.

Tickets for Mayweather - De La Hoya sold out in three hours and the gate grossed $19m, easily beating the previous best for Tyson – Holyfield. The hype was planet sized too with HBO producing a four part documentary entitled *De La Hoya-Mayweather*

24/7. Both fighters were shown in training with the final episode screened two days before the fight.

A typical twist to the story was whether Golden Boy would be trained by Mayweather Sr. He was estranged from Floyd Jr and had been training De La Hoya since 2001. In true Mayweather style Floyd Sr demanded a huge fee, $2m , to train De La Hoya for the fight with his son but this was turned down. Instead he was offered $500,000 plus another $500,000 if De La Hoya won. This was not acceptable and the De La Hoya camp went with Freddie Roach, Manny Pacquiao's regular trainer.

Floyd Sr was reconciled with his son before the fight but played no part in his training. Uncle Roger Mayweather carried on instead – even though Floyd Sr wanted to take over. From the start De La Hoya took the action to Floyd but then a familiar pattern was began to show.

Just like Zab Judah, Oscar was not throwing enough jabs and for the same reason. When he did he got caught with heavy rights. In the fight Mayweather connected with nearly twice as many punches as De La Hoya, 207 against 122. The longer the fight went, the more he dominated - even though De La Hoya's stamina held up well and he never stopped looking for an opening.

It was a surprise when a split decision was announced, most thought Mayweather had won easily.

The pre-fight hype had a storyline of 'Will this fight save boxing, will it be the last great fight?' The hope was that it would attract casual fans back to the sport and combat the attractions of martial arts. It probably did that but the contest should be judged for what it was. Two great practitioners putting on a non-stop display of skilful fighting.

De La Hoya looked good against Mayweather but his next fight was probably one too many. He was outclassed by Pacquiao who had Freddie Roach in his corner. Roach said afterwards, "We knew we were going to win after the first round, De La Hoya can't pull the trigger any more."

"What A Fluke!"

Jokey crack from Ricky Hatton after Floyd Mayweather caught him with a checked left hook he never saw that knocked him off his feet

Money Mayweather versus Hitman Hatton was the meeting of two undefeated fighters with impressive and similar records. Both were world champions with over 40 fights and there was only a year's difference in their ages. But after that came huge differences in styles, skills and life styles. Mayweather, the teetotal gym fanatic who was never out of training. Hatton, a man who enjoyed booze, nightlife and fast food binges in between fights – before he went back to the gym.

Mayweather the classic defensive fighter, fast and fluent with a knockout punch in both hands. A man who liked to use the ring and his speed to wear opponents down. Hatton, a fighter with a good chin prepared to take a few punches who loved to work inside and also had a knockout punch in both hands.

It was a clash of styles, temperaments and boxing cultures. Two proud men who declared they had nothing to prove to the world – but a lot to each other. One of the telling statistics was the length of their arms. Hatton was giving away six inches to Mayweather, he needed to be up close and went into the fight thinking he would have the edge there.

In the early rounds Hatton looked the dominant fighter but as ever, it was Mayweather landing the scoring punches. Left and right combinations plus thunderous rights that snapped Hatton's head back.

Even so Hatton competed well. In the first he caught Mayweather with a stinging jab that knocked him out of his stride. The Hitman came out with constant aggression and a determination to come forward, no matter what Mayweather threw. His tactics made Money clutch and hold. But in the third one of Mayweather's rights opened up a cut over Hatton's right eye.

Gradually Mayweather's movement stole the energy from Hatton as he was forced to chase the faster man. The end began in the 9th when Mayweather landed 15 left jabs as Hatton rushed in again and again. The punishment didn't stop Hatton's fans singing but the end came in the next round. A blur of a left hook caught Hatton as he came flailing in. He went down then got up on wobbling legs. Mayweather was onto him and for once Hatton retreated. Then, as he stumbled towards a corner he fell, exhausted. It was all over.

Afterwards Hatton admitted Mayweather was too fast, too clever on the night. He claimed to have met bigger punchers but it was Mayweather who left him flat on his back for the first time in his professional career.

The distinguished trainer Emmanuel Steward who was commentating on the fight said Ricky Hatton brought out the best in Mayweather, forcing him take chances and show more of his skills than he had in a long time. It was a superb fight between two contrasting fighters. Speaking later Money said he had nothing more to prove and this time he really was retiring. He did – for twenty one months.

Mayweather Wasn't Punching Stats – He Was Punching Marquez And Mosley

For his comeback fight Mayweather chose Juan Manuel Marquez, a Mexican hero, lightweight title holder and former featherweight champion. It was a catch weight contest and Mayweather clearly had a size advantage.

But the Mexican had basic problems from the first round, he was always struggling to get close enough to Mayweather to land his heavy combinations. The punch stats said it all, Marquez landed only 12% of the 583 punches he threw.

The contrast was huge, Mayweather landed 59%, 290 out of 493, a strike rate that won him every round. The fight went the distance but there was only ever going to be one winner with Mayweather's foot speed, hand speed and reaction time taking him out of trouble every time Marquez made a lunge. Then there was the shoulder roll and the body sway. Mayweather was just too hard to hit and Marquez joined the long line of fighters shaking their heads at the end of a contest and telling the truth, "He's just too fast."

But that's not the way Shane Moseley saw it from the ringside.

He thought he could catch Mayweather and had the punch to put him away. But the stat that really interested him was the payday. At 38 he was thinking the Mayweather gift for making money was just what he needed. There was the usual pre-match circus with a debate between the two refereed by Max Kellerman and the fight was made.

A match with Pacquiao had previously been talked up but fell through over Floyd's drug testing demands. Pacquiao said he would agree to a blood test if it wasn't held too close to the fight. As the smaller man he claimed a blood test then would give Mayweather an advantage.

So that fight was off – and Mosley was in. Happily so, he was guaranteed $7M plus a share of the TV receipts. Floyd was on a cool $22M.

Mosley started very aggressively and his theories about landing a big punch looked good in the second when he caught Mayweather with a right hand that rocked him. Floyd's knees sagged and his composure was nearly gone but the Mayweather boxing instincts kicked in and he grabbed Mosley, hanging onto his unbeaten record. It nearly went in that moment. Later in the round Mosley caught him again – but that was as close as he came to rewriting the script.

Mayweather won every round after that, landing 208 punches to Mosley's 92. After the seventh round Mosley's corner told him to forget about going for the big shot, he had to throw more punches. But like every other fighter before him, Mosley knew that trying to box Mayweather simply opened him up to faster hands.

Floyd won by boxing – not trading punches. He dictated but also giving the fans what they wanted, a fast all action contest. There was no dispute about the winner and afterwards Mosley said he couldn't land another big one, "He was too quick and I was too tight."

"He's Just Been On A Learning Experience"

Announcer introducing Victor Ortiz at the post fight press conference

That was one way of putting it and to his credit Ortiz didn't go overboard on the bad side of what had just happened in the ring with Floyd Mayweather. To say the ending was unexpected doesn't do it justice, this was drama on a par with someone suddenly pulling a gun in the middle of an ordinary argument.

Ortiz came into the ring as the younger man by 10 years but with a world welterweight title to defend. This was Mayweather's first fight for 16 months and pre-fight rumors that he was having hand trouble were later confirmed. The first three rounds all went to Mayweather and it was obvious his defensive skills were frustrating Ortiz. As usual Mayweather's accurate punches were scoring points but Ortiz was missing badly. The Money Man had twice the strike rate although the punches weren't hurting Ortiz particularly.

It was all very frustrating for Ortiz. But in the fourth round he seemed to rally and drove Mayweather onto the ropes. He did it again and with Mayweather's back to the ropes suddenly grabbed him round the neck and pulled him onto a head butt. It was out in the open, blatant, and Ortiz immediately realised he had made a major mistake. The referee ordered them to break and they did. Ortiz hugged Mayweather in apology and even kissed him on the cheek. They touched gloves and Ortiz looked towards the referee, checking it was OK to fight on. His guard was very much down at this point.

Mistake. Mayweather didn't hesitate, they had already touched gloves and with Ortiz looking away – Floyd landed a blistering combination. After the first punch Ortiz was in shock and still looking towards the referee. The second shot, a hard right straight to the chin – took him out.

It all happened so quickly even the referee wasn't watching, he was checking with officials that they had seen his one point deduction for the head butt. The next thing the ref saw was Ortiz going down. When he hit the floor the ref started counting but by now Ortiz was already an ex-champion. He tried to get up but didn't really know what was going on as the referee counted him out. It was all over and even after they got him back to his corner Ortiz still wasn't clear about what happened.

He made a mistake and paid for it. The referee's instruction at the beginning of every fight is, "Protect yourself at all times." Ortiz clearly didn't.

Afterwards Mayweather finally lost his cool and patience with HBO commentator Larry Merchant in their post fight interview. Merchant was goading him all the way through. His entire focus was on Ortiz being a flawed opponent and Mayweather's 'unfair' knockout after they touched gloves.

Correctly saying that he never got a "Fair shake" from Merchant, Floyd stormed off after an expletive aimed at the commentator. Merchant's unbelievable response was that if he was 50 years younger he would "whup Mayweather's ass." A ludicrous remark that did him and HBO no credit at all. It simply confirmed that Merchant never stopped trying – and failing - to bring the Money Man down.

"It's the hurt business, it's boxing, we're there to get it in"
Floyd Mayweather

Mayweather's fight against Miguel Cotto may have been his best performance so far. Cotto was a former 147lb champion, dangerous and durable, always up for the fight.

Critics before the fight were saying that Floyd was at his best moving round the ring, dancing in to throw combinations, using his shoulder roll and footwork to get out of trouble. Therefore Cotto's best chance was to crowd the unbeaten champion, cut off his ring space, make him go toe to toe. Try and trap him on the ropes.

That may be good strategic planning. The only problem was, Floyd never read the script. There was a round when Cotto did have him backed onto the ropes but Floyd made it work for him. He held Cotto off, measured him up and banged in three straight lefts without reply. Right through the fight he was scoring with both hands. In a later round he rocked Cotto with a hard right then whipped in a left hook that made him cover up and back off. That was the pattern of the fight. Cotto did land some good punches but often Mayweather was moving away, taking the sting out of them. Then in the last round Mayweather almost had Cotto down.

The other factor on non-stop display was Floyd's stamina. He kept going, throwing his point scoring punches then sliding out of trouble, tiring Cotto, making him chase. Fast hands, fast feet – and a fast brain.

It was a unanimous decision but a tremendous, compelling fight. Afterwards Cotto was not downbeat. "It was a good fight, you win some, lose some, but it was a good fight." For consolation he had his best ever purse, $8m. Floyd took $32m in what was one of Nevada's biggest ever gates.

"You're blowin' it son, you're blowin' it"

Angelo Dundee

Spoken by one of the sport's most famous characters to Sugar Ray Leonard, this phrase has gone into the subconscious of boxers, trainers and fans. The occasion was the fight to unify the welterweight championship in 1981 between Leonard and Thomas Hearns. Angelo Dundee, who trained Ali and was in the corner for all of his career, began with middleweight champion Carmen Basilio back in the fifties. In total he trained fifteen world champions. Dundee's experience, ring cunning and motivational skills were prized by his fighters.

The fight to unify the world welterweight titles between Leonard and Hearns in 1981 was a classic between two men who could box and mix it. It swung backwards and forwards but by the twelve Hearns was in front and Dundee thought Leonard was letting Hearns dictate. Between the 12th and 13th rounds he had a few hard words with his fighter. He said, "What you doing, you nuts? You got to move, speed, you're fighting his fight. Pick it up! You're not slow like this guy."

But only his final words, "You're blowin' it son, you're blowin it" were caught on camera. The point was, the words worked. Leonard went out to attack, turned the fight his way and Hearns was stopped in the 14th when Sugar Ray put him through the ropes.

Mayweather's corner is always a family affair but even if Dundee had been in there – he wouldn't have needed to make that kind of intervention. Floyd doesn't 'fight the other guy's fight'. So far he has had the speed, discipline and power to impose himself, fight his own way. In one of his final interviews before his death in 2013 Dundee said Mayweather had been to see him in Florida. "I like the guy, he was joking around. He kept saying to me, 'You're blowin it son, you're blowin' it.' "

New World Title For Mayweather : Undisputed Pay Per View Champion

Floyd's next fight after Cotto was with Robert Guerro but the bigger news was that this was the first of a new six fight, Pay Per View Deal he signed with Showtime Networks. His last three fights had produced an average of 1.4m Pay Per View buys and if Money can maintain his form – there's plenty more where that came from.

The Money Man gives himself an even better deal by acting as his own promoter through his company Mayweather Promotions. He collects from tickets, ppv and sponsorship while he pays costs and his opponent's purse. The days of promoters calling the shots are way behind Team Mayweather, he has put himself on top of the pile. But of course, everything hangs on his ring performances.

He could be looking at fight guarantees of $200 million for the six fights with pay per view revenues on top of that. According to Forbes Magazine, in June 2012 Money was the world's highest paid athlete. He leaves stars like Michael Jordan and Tiger Woods behind.

For the Guerrero fight Floyd had his father back in his corner. Part of his thinking was that he had taken more punishment than usual against Cotto and he wanted to get back to the defensive control that worked so well for him for most of his career. As Floyd Senior put it, "The less you get hit the longer you last."

Before he stepped into the ring Guerrero had not lost for eight years. His calling card is The Ghost, his speed makes him elusive and his record shows 31 wins with 18 KO's. But this was not his night. Every time The Ghost started throwing punches it was Floyd who disappeared. When he reappeared he was jabbing Guerrero any time he felt like it and throwing right hands that wobbled him in the eighth.

Even at 36 Mayweather's speed puts him into a different league. When Guerrero was asked afterwards if he thought Mayweather could be beaten he said "Sure, if you can catch him."

That's What The Great Joe Louis Said About Sonny Liston

After his win over Canelo Alvarez in the next fight many respected boxing critics were saying the only thing that was going to beat Floyd Mayweather Jr was old age. Which is exactly what long term heavyweight king Joe Louis said about Sonny Liston after the Big Bear's campaign of the late fifties and early sixties. Sonny was knocking over everyone put in front of him - and leaving them on the floor. That includes Cleveland Williams, Zora Folley and World Champion Floyd Patterson who went in one round - twice.

Then Sonny met Ali, or Cassius as he was then.

So is there an unknown Ali out there waiting for Floyd? Maybe, maybe not but what we can say for certain is that Floyd is no Sonny. He doesn't have a problem with training, he enjoys it. The Money Man doesn't drink and doesn't socialise with the Mob. He doesn't do drugs, although to be fair, neither did Sonny. Old Stone Face was accused of drug use after his mysterious death which was put down to an overdose. An overdose of the Mob more likely but that's another story.

If there is an another threat as potentially dangerous as Ali waiting – apart from Pacquiao of course - nobody has spotted him yet. But everyone is looking and nobody harder than Floyd himself. He knows he won't last forever and maybe he can find the new Floyd himself. His wheeling and dealing shows he is as smart with business strategy as he is in the ring. Long term his plan could be to find the next big talent then use Team Mayweather to train, manage and promote him.

Floyd's fight with Saul Alvarez took him to 45 fights – and 45 wins. If the numbers are impressive the skills on show against Alvarez took fans and purists alike to new levels of appreciation. It was a master class of defence and offence. The way Mayweather slipped out of trouble time after time totally frustrated the Mexican hero. His thousands of supporters in the stadium roared him on non-stop but there was a spell in the 7th when Alvarez simply stayed on the ropes. He could do no more than cover up as Mayweather held him rooted to the spot.

Jab after jab fixed him. They were followed by hooks and uppercuts that punished him. The only way to describe him was bemused. The shots came in so fast Alvarez could do no more than put his gloves up, and cover up. Afterwards he acknowledged Mayweather's performance saying, "He's a great fighter, intelligent." Shrugging his shoulders he put the problem simply, "I just couldn't find him."

Then he delivered the bad news that nearly every opponent so far has discovered. "There is no solution." Mayweather landed with almost twice as many punches, even though Alvarez threw more. Afterwards Mayweather praised Alvarez as a great Mexican champion but said if he'd started his attack earlier he could have taken him out.

The rewards reflected the status of both fighters. Alvarez had a big pay day with a purse of $5M. Mayweather took $41M plus pay per view. Says it all really.

Mayweather has already fought and beaten 20 world champions. So who can we compare him to? Amongst present day fighters it's Pacquiao of course. But from the past the obvious candidate is Sugar Ray Robinson. Fighting in very different times, both socially and financially, the great Sugar Ray had a twenty five year career with 200 contests. He won 173 and, at a time when there were less weight categories than today, defeated 16 world champions. In 2007

ESPN voted him the greatest fighter in history. Many who know boxing would agree.

But in a comparison between Robinson and Mayweather one of the most intriguing aspects is the six fights and intense rivalry Sugar Ray had with Jake LaMotta. They give us a tantalising glimpse of what could have been in a different Mayweather and Pacquiao story.

Could Mayweather and Pacquiao have been like Robinson and LaMotta?

Robinson was the defensive dancer with a knockout in both hands, LaMotta, a Raging Bull of attack who never stopped coming forward. A promoter's dream of a match. It could be a mirror image of a Mayweather – Pacman promotion. That's why there are still headlines every week about the chances of it happening. One big difference is that Robinson and LaMotta began their rivalry at the start of their careers. Today Mayweather and Pacquiao have developed into mature, highly experienced fighters. They are well down the road. If they meet it will not be the same fight as the first Robinson – LaMotta contest - but still well worth the wait.

Sugar Ray and Jake LaMotta fought six times with Robinson winning five and Lamotta one but they were a lot closer than that record suggests. Several of the later contests could have gone either way and as Lamotta himself has said, "You don't fight each other that often unless the fights are very, very close."

Lamotta who is still around at the age of 90 says "There's no question Robinson was the greatest fighter who ever lived. He was unbeaten in his first 100 fights – then I beat him."

Straight away those figures tell you everything about the big boxing differences. Back in the forties when Lamotta beat Robinson the sport was mainstream, main event, crowd stopping. They fought each other twice in one month – a situation that wouldn't even be thought about today when boxing has slipped down to niche status.

For one thing today's blue chip fighters don't need to fight that often. Their finances are very different with Mayweather getting guaranteed purses of $40M. In contrast, even after his stellar career, Robinson died broke. He had been forced to make a comeback when he was in his forties.

In their first fight in Madison Square Gardens Robinson beat Lamotta but Jake had him down in the first round. That convinced the fans they wanted to see more and the first re-match was arranged. LaMotta was one of the first 'bully' fighters who tried to crowd his opponent at all times and took punches so well he was never knocked off his feet throughout his career. His record was eighty three wins with thirty knock outs.

Each one of their six fights was a sell out. LaMotta who would later perform as a stand up comedian joked, "I fought Sugar so often I nearly got diabetes."

For the second fight LaMotta went to Robinson's home town of Detroit and won a cracking fight. In the same month they fought again – and Robinson came out the winner. Immediately afterwards Robinson went into the army and toured briefly with Joe Louis, entertaining the troops during World War Two.

Both LaMotta and Robinson came from the traditional boxing backgrounds of tough childhoods. Robinson danced on the streets of Detroit to earn money, LaMotta was in daily street fights in the Bronx. Like Mayweather, Sugar Ray spent his youth in gyms, Joe Louis was an early hero and he graduated to a Golden Gloves championship at featherweight.

The title 'pound for pound the best' that Floyd has held for so long was invented to describe Sugar Ray. He won it with the same fast hands and dancing feet -

but a harder punch in both hands than Floyd. Robinson was welterweight champion from 1946 to '51 and between '51 and '60 he won the middleweight championship five times.

One of the biggest differences between the boxing times of Robinson/LaMotta and Mayweather/Pacquiao is that from the forties to the late sixties much of boxing was controlled by the Mafia. Robinson had made his name before the Mob won near total control so he wasn't so badly affected until his later career. But LaMotta was held back from championship fights for a long time because he wouldn't co-operate with them. He refused to throw fights that would have made big money for the Mob in betting scams.

Eventually in desperation and knowing it was the only way he was going to get a title shot, LaMotta gave in and agreed to throw a fight against Billy Fox. But LaMotta was always his own man and in the fight he didn't 'pretend' well enough and the decision for Fox brought big controversy. Yet the Mob controlled so much of boxing that LaMotta got his shot at the middleweight title. He fought French champion Marcel Cerdan for a purse of $100K and won. At last he was King – but Sugar Ray was still around.

There had to be a final, and sixth fight. Robinson was finding it harder to make welterweight so he moved up and they met in Chicago in 1951 for the title. There are many contenders for fight of the century, this is definitely one of them. During training Robinson said his plan would be to let LaMotta punch himself out in the early rounds then take over. The original version of Ali's 'Rope a Dope' strategy against George Foreman. LaMotta only ever had one plan To go out and slug, take as many punches as he had to so he could land his.

For the first eight rounds LaMotta came out, fighting in his usual crouching style, taking the left jabs and right hooks Robinson threw but landing smashing crosses of his own. He was ahead on points until, in the ninth, he started to tire and Robinson unloaded his own attack. Fast combinations poured in with LaMotta still taking everything but getting slower and slower.

The next four rounds gave the fight its name, 'St Valentine's Day Massacre' after the killings organised by Al Capone. Robinson was hitting his man at will, smashing big right hooks into him. The slaughter continued until the 13th with LaMotta refusing to go down, not matter what Robinson threw. Eventually, and long after it would have been stopped today, the referee stepped in.

Jake LaMotta may have lost to Robinson but he started the process that eventually led to the untangling of the Mob from boxing. He testified that he had thrown the fight with Fox and confirmed what was open knowledge in the boxing community. Speaking for many fighters, former middleweight champion Carl (Bobo) Olson said boxers worked hard for their living while gangsters took everything and it was time they were out of the sport.

Can The Pound For Pound Man Punch Out Pacquiao?

Let's assume the Mayweather/Pacquiao fight is made and every sign – each one with a dollar bill attached – says it will eventually. Could it be a story like Robinson and LaMotta, though surely not with as many episodes? If so the scenario is looking good for Floyd. His talents, skills and speed seem to have longer lasting qualities than the Pacman's endurance. The Money Man's dancing feet are still there, positioning him to land jab after jab followed by crisp right hands. But while Jake LaMotta was able to take that sort of treatment from Robinson and stay there, the way Juan Miguel Marquez put Pacquiao away in their last fight shivered the Pacman's army of fans, right down to their bones.

One second Manny was boring in, aiming to land a right. Then it looked as if he was leading with a wide open chin and Marquez caught him with a belter right on the button. Down he went and down he stayed.

Marquez was leaping round the ring, he knew the Pacman would not get up. Compare that to his fight with Floyd Mayweather when the best he could do, for his own pride's sake, was hang on for the last two rounds. He caught punch after punch but like LaMotta against Robinson, he would not go down.

Floyd Mayweather is just as determined to hang onto his unbeaten record. He doesn't want to be another top fighter with a string of world titles. Mayweather wants to be remembered as one of the best of all time. He doesn't use the Ali word, the 'Greatest' but that is his motivation, his focus. It's what he takes into the ring for every fight. For seventeen years he has been working in the gym, hyping his fights, piling up the cash. He has no intention of being left like Sugar Ray with nothing to show for a stratospheric career.

Sugar Ray pioneered a certain style, and lifestyle, that Floyd has picked up on. Sugar was famous for his 'entourage' – the people who travelled with him. The term was invented in Paris when he arrived with his masseur, hairdresser, a man who whistled while he trained, a secretary, voice coach, several beautiful women and a dwarf mascot. And a Flamingo pink Cadillac.

Floyd has Team Mayweather – but there is a vital difference. The members of Team Mayweather all have important jobs. They train him, help him with management, advise him inside and outside the ring.

They work on sponsorship deals, organise ticket sales, look after merchandising, keep his promotional company running smoothly. There are accountants, tax experts and lawyers. No training whistlers and no dwarf mascot.

The key word around Team Mayweather is focus. Everything is devoted to what happens in the ring, it's attention to detail – and an eye to the future. But naturally there's fun time too. One car dealer says Floyd bought 88 cars from him and he's still looking. There are beautiful women around too but come fight time it is strictly business.

Sugar Ray said boxing was all about rhythm. For him every punch started with the heart and "If that's not in rhythm you're in trouble." Floyd has a different theory, he thinks if a boxer has a rhythm the other guy can pick up on it – and he's in trouble. That's why Floyd mixes it up. Nobody knows what's coming next but you can be sure - it will be dangerous.

Let's leave the last word to the great Angelo Dundee and what he learned over sixty years around fighters. "You've got to be a special person. Boxing only works with certain people. It's a tough hustle."

Exactly. That's why so many people admire good fighters and Floyd is simply . . . better than good

Made in the USA
Lexington, KY
04 May 2014